THE FLY

For Sophie,
my little fruit fly

Text and illustrations copyright © 2014 by Elise Gravel
Copyright for the French edition: Elise Gravel and Les éditions de la courte échelle inc., 2012
Paperback edition published in 2016 by Tundra Books, an imprint of Penguin Random House Canada
Young Readers, a Penguin Random House Company

Library and Archives Canada Cataloguing in Publication

Gravel, Elise
[Mouche. English]
    The fly / Elise Gravel.

(Disgusting critters)
Translation of: La mouche.
Previously published by Tundra Books, 2014.
ISBN 978-1-101-91840-1 (paperback)

    1. Flies—Juvenile literature. I. Title. II. Title: Mouche.
English. III. Series: Gravel, Élise. Disgusting critters.

QL533.2.G7213 2016   j595.77   C2015-904001-9

Published simultaneously in the United States of America by Tundra Books of Northern New York,
an imprint of Penguin Random House Canada Young Readers, a Penguin Random House Company

Library of Congress Control Number: 2013940756

English edition edited by Samantha Swenson
Designed by Elise Gravel and Tundra Books
The artwork in this book was rendered digitally
Printed and bound in China

www.penguinrandomhouse.ca

5 6 7 8   23 22 21 20

Elise Gravel

THE FLY

tundra

Let me introduce you
to a very special guy.

HERE'S

THE FLY.

There are more than

100,000
SPECIES OF FLIES

in the world.

The green bottle fly

Pff! Who are you calling green?

The blue bottle fly

I feel sad sometimes.

The fruit fly

Also known as
Drosophila.

The housefly

He's the hero
of this book.

Because I'm the king
of the trash heap!

The housefly is a member of the
MUSCIDAE
FAMILY.

Mom
Muscidae

Dad
Muscidae

Baby
Muscidae

We don't call him the

HOUSEFLY

because he's a pet, like a dog or cat,
but because he likes to get inside our

HOUSES.

Hey, I'm not a DOG!

The housefly is found in every country in the world. Houseflies like humans because we offer them a warm place to live and lots of

GARBAGE TO EAT.

The housefly is gray, with black stripes on his back, and his body is

COVERED WiTH HAiR.

That means a lot of shaving!

The housefly measures from 0.2 to 0.3 inches (5 to 8 millimeters) long. The female is slightly bigger than the male.

The housefly's eyes are red and have many tiny flat surfaces that allow him to see in all directions at the same time.

JONATHAN!
I told you not to snack before dinner.

Thanks to little

BUBBLES OF LIQUID

at the ends of his feet, the housefly
can walk on walls or even on the

CEILING.

It's pretty cool,
but it's not easy to
play soccer up here.

The housefly uses his tube-shaped mouth to suck up his food. He can only eat

LIQUID FOODS, or just LIQUID,

so he spits or vomits a bit of digestive fluid on his meal to soften it.

The fly has really

DISGUSTING TASTE iN FOOD.

The female fly can lay over a hundred eggs at a time. From the egg comes a maggot, which then turns into a pupa, which then becomes a fly.

 1 MAGGOT

 2 PUPA

3 FLY

The fly can be eaten by other insects, such as spiders, or by birds or fish. The fly lives between

15 AND 30 DAYS.

I want you home before ten o'clock, Josephine. Understood?

Because he walks on garbage and gross stuff like poo, the fly can carry

GERMS

and cause hundreds of

DISEASES.

Good morning.
You ordered a flu?

So next time a fly wants to share your food, make sure he washes

HIS HANDS.

You wouldn't have rotten mayo for the fries, by any chance?